The BuzzyLuvz
Practice Kindness

Lesson 6: Be thankful

by MARNIE HOWARD

illustrated by Eric Austin

Dedicated to my nephews Max & Lander

Copyright 2012 by Marnie Howard. All rights reserved. No part of this book may be reproduced, scanned, or distributed in any printed or electronic form without written permission from the author, except for brief passages included in a review. For information:
P.O. box 192423, Miami Beach, FL 33119

The BuzzyLuvz bees follow their hearts to lead them to those in need of an act of kindness.

Lesson 6: Be thankful
Be someone who is appreciative that something or someone exists.

BUZZ ONE

Thank you parents for taking care of me.

BUZZ TWO

Thank you brother and sister for being a mentor.

BUZZ THREE

Thank you pets for playing with me.

BUZZ FOUR

Thank you rainbows for all of your beautiful colors.

BUZZ FIVE

Thank you flowers for all of your sweet smelling scents.

BUZZ SIX

Thank you rain for helping the grass and flowers grow.

BUZZ SEVEN

Thank you hugs for making me feel loved.

BUZZ EIGHT

Thank you sunshine
for warmth and light.

BUZZ NINE

Thank you balloons for making parties more fun.

BUZZ TEN

Thank you best friend for always keeping my secrets.

BUZZ ELEVEN

Thank you eyes for allowing me to see all the beautiful things in the world.

BUZZ TWELVE

Thank you voice for allowing me to speak and sing.

BUZZ THIRTEEN

Thank you tongue for allowing me to taste sweet treats.

BUZZ FOURTEEN

Thank you fingers for allowing me to touch fuzzy teddy bears.

BUZZ FIFTEEN

Thank you empathy for teaching me how to treat others.

BUZZ SIXTEEN

Thank you movies for making me laugh.

BUZZ SEVENTEEN

Thank you books for all the great adventures.

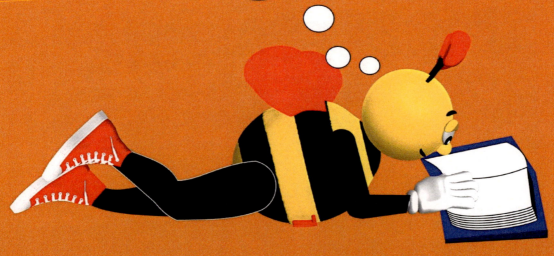

BUZZ EIGHTEEN

Thank you ears for letting me hear beautiful music.

BUZZ NINETEEN

Thank you teacher for teaching me so many important lessons.

BUZZ TWENTY

Thank you trees for providing shade on hot summer days.

Follow your heart and pass on kindness to others.

The Bee Kindhearted Effect
The flutter of a bee's wings will create
a flood of kindness that can be felt in
schools and homes across the world.

THE END

Made in the USA
Middletown, DE
20 May 2016